Nellie Bly

Published in the United States of America by Cherry Lake Publishing
Ann Arbor, Michigan
www.cherrylakepublishing.com

Reading Adviser: Marla Conn, MS, Ed, Literacy Specialist, Read-Ability, Inc.
Book Designer: Jennifer Wahi
Illustrator: Jeff Bane

Photo Credits: © Everett Historical/Shutterstock.com, 5; © Arturs Budkevics, 7; Thurston, George H (1876)/
Wikimedia/Public Domain, 9, 22; © LSE Library/Flickr, 11; © Dave Miller Flickr, 13; © National Archives Catalog/
Local ID. 69-RP-403/Hine, Lewis Wickes/1874-1940, 15; © University of Pennsylvania Library [1887]/Wikimedia, 17;
© Library of Congress/Reproduction No. LC-USZ61-2126, 19, 23; © Library of Congress/Reproduction No.
LC-USZ62-59923, 21; Cover, 1, 6, 16, 18, Jeff Bane; Various frames throughout, ©Shutterstock Images

Library of Congress Cataloging-in-Publication Data

Names: Spiller, Sara, author. | Bane, Jeff, 1957- illustrator.
Title: Nellie Bly / author, Sara Spiller ; illustrator, Jeff Bane.
Description: Ann Arbor, Michigan : Cherry Lake Publishing, [2019] | Series:
   My itty-bitty bio | Audience: K-003.
Identifiers: LCCN 2018034520| ISBN 9781534142732 (hardcover) | ISBN
   9781534139299 (paperback) | ISBN 9781534140493 (pdf) | ISBN 9781534141698
   (hosted ebook)
Subjects: LCSH: Bly, Nellie, 1864-1922--Juvenile literature. | Women
   journalists--United States--Biography--Juvenile literature. | LCGFT:
   Biographies. | Readers (Publications)
Classification: LCC PN4874.B59 S65 2019 | DDC 070.92--dc23
LC record available at https://lccn.loc.gov/2018034520

Printed in the United States of America
Corporate Graphics

About the author: Sara Spiller is a native of the state of Michigan. She enjoys reading comic books and hanging out with her cats.

About the illustrator: Jeff Bane and his two business partners own a studio along the American River in Folsom, California, home of the 1849 Gold Rush. When Jeff's not sketching or illustrating for clients, he's either swimming or kayaking in the river to relax.

I was born in 1864. My name was Elizabeth Jane Cochran.

My father died when I was young. My mother and I did not have much money.

I read a newspaper. A man wrote that women should not have jobs.

They should stay at home. They should not earn their own money.

How were women treated in the past?

I wrote a **response**. I said women should have jobs if they wanted one.

My response shocked people. That newspaper gave me a job!

I wrote for the newspaper.
My **pen name** was Nellie Bly.
I wrote about the **oppressed**.
I wrote about the poor. I wrote
about women's rights.

Why would someone use a fake name?

I did things **undercover**.
I acted like someone else.
I wrote about what I saw.

I worked in a **sweatshop**.
The women working there were
treated badly. I wrote about this.
Everyone read it.

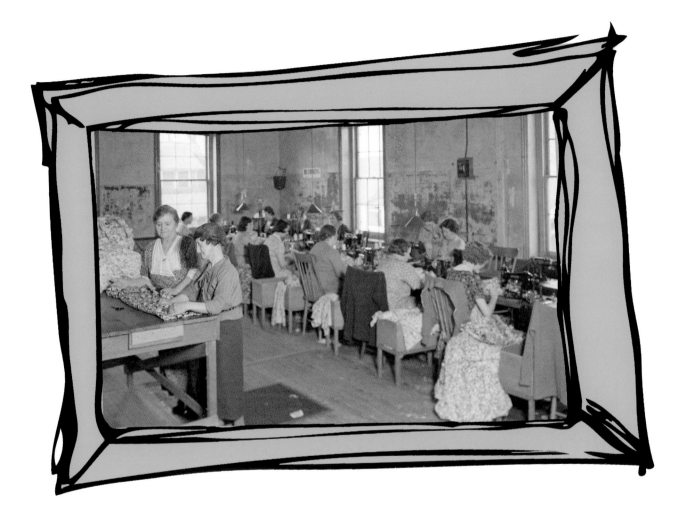

I was undercover at a hospital. I pretended I was sick. What I wrote helped make changes. Laws were made to help the people I wrote about.

IN THE INTELLIGENCE OFFICE.

What would you do undercover?

I went around the world in 72 days!

I became famous for this.

I died in 1922. My writing **exposed** problems.

I showed people that women can be writers!

What would you like to ask me?

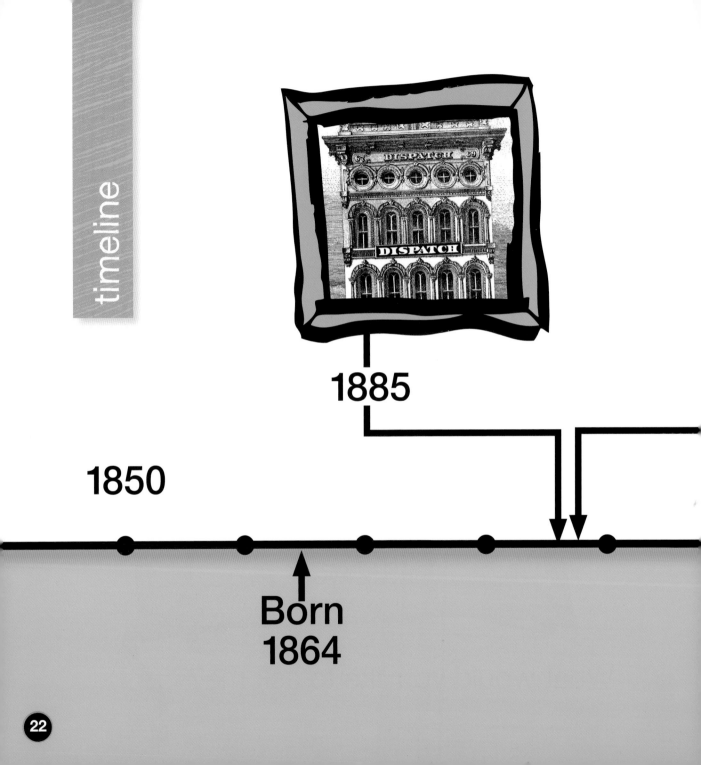

1885

1850

Born
1864

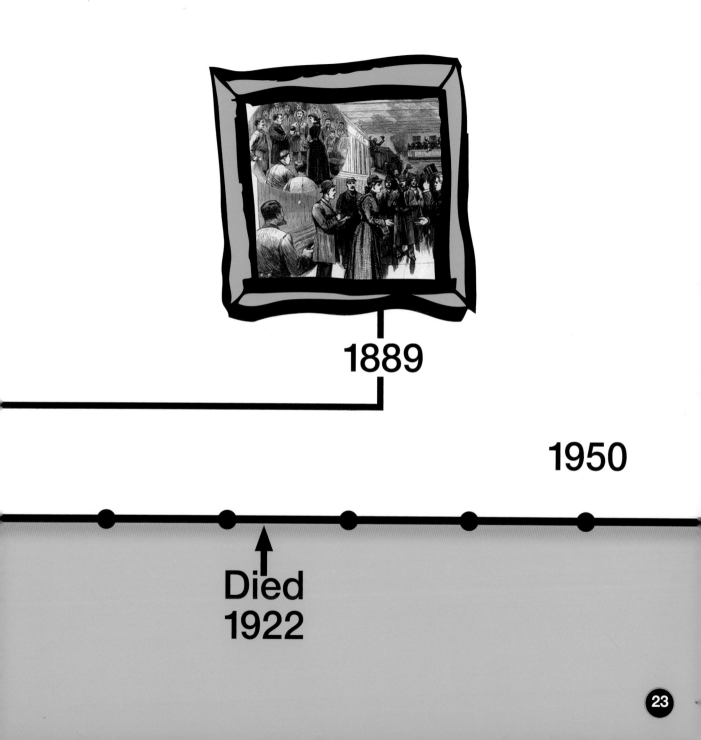

1889

1950

Died
1922

glossary

exposed (ik-SPOZED) to find out and share a secret about someone or something

oppressed (uh-PRESD) people treated badly by those in power

pen name (PEN NAME) a fake name used to keep a person safe

response (rih-SPAHNS) a reply someone writes or says

sweatshop (SWET-shahp) a factory where workers make very little money and work long hours

undercover (uhn-dur-KUHV-ur) done in secret

index